More Inspirations of God

by

Jerry Barfield

www.rdtalleybooks.com

Las Vegas, Nevada

The Holy Bible version referenced in this book is the King James Version.

Cover Designed by Michela Fellows

ISBN: 978-1-957294-02-5

Copyright © 2022 by Jerry Barfield

All rights reserved. No part of this publication may be reproduced, distributed, or transmitted in any form or by any means, including photocopying, recording, or other electronic or mechanical methods without the prior written permission of the publisher. For permission requests, solicit the publisher via the address or website below.

R.D. Talley Books Publishing, LLC
P.O. Box 271029
Las Vegas, Nevada 89127
www.rdtalleybooks.com

Dedication/Special Thanks

This book is dedicated to three people:

First, to the person who made a nobody into a somebody: Jesus Christ.

Second, to the first person who showed me who Jesus Christ really is:
Bertha W. Barfield (1892-1983)
Thanks Grandma.

Third, to those who truly believe that what I do is truly God's work.

Thank You and God Bless You!

Table of Contents

Introduction 7
Why The Rib? 8
The 4 Bad D's vs. The 4 Good D's 9
Waymaker 12
Who's World Is This? Really? 18
The 5th Bad D vs. The 5th Good D 20
But Whose Side Are You On? 22
Please Don't Cry 25
Send Me 27
Sent To Save 30
Saved By Grace 33
I Have The Power 35
How Sweet It Is 38
Holiday Intermission 40
Whole Heart 41
God's Hammer 44
No Confusion 47
Count It 49
The Fulfilling Power of God 51
It's Only My Pride 53
Like A Tree 56
The Power of Praise 59
Prisoner or Free Man: Which One Are You? 61

Hiding In Plain Sight 64
Have A Life 67
Believe and See Not 70

Introduction

Messiah calls, and again I have answered. I praise Him, once again, to hear that small still voice that leads me in the life and to help in the walk of all the saints of God. Once again, I bid you greetings in the name of Jesus Christ, that once again He has stretched forth His mighty hand over you and that God gives you the understanding that is needed to be used for His glory.

And now this time as last, but with a different twist, may these inspirations be a revelation towards your edification, regardless of your denomination!

Thank you and God bless you!

Why the Rib?
Proverbs 18:22

One day as I was speaking to the Lord, I asked him, "Lord, of all the places you could've created woman, why did you use a rib?" The Lord told me, "My son, before I answer that question, I'll let you know why I didn't make her from another part."

"I didn't make her from your back, for then she would be behind you. I didn't make her from your chest, so she wouldn't be in front of you. I didn't make her from your head, then she would be over you, and I didn't make her from your feet, so then she would be under you. My son, I made her from your rib because she is your helpmate and what better place for a helpmate to come from than beside you."

As Solomon had said in Proverbs 18:22, "Whoso findeth a wife, findeth a good thing, and obtaineth favor of the Lord." So remember, as long as you are with her, not only do you have a "good thing", but you've found favor in God, and that's why she came from the rib.

The 4 Bad D's vs. The 4 Good D's
Psalms 119:38

It seems that no matter what good we do in life, something bad always happen. But those who are in love with the Lord knows that there has to be something to bring you down, so you can rise up stronger in Christ. He will take the bad out of your life and put in something good, and I'm here to show you those things in my life.

First, we will deal with the bad D's, which starts-off with death. When my mother passed away, I didn't have the understanding of it as I currently do, now that I'm one with Christ. Meaning that although death is a permanent state, when we have Christ, we can all be together once again to rejoice in Him.

The second D is for departure because when you're living to be one in God, a lot of things and people depart from you, especially people that you had called your friends. When God elevates us in our walk with Him, He shows us that some people won't be able to stay connected with us. The reasons for this are various, but it usually means that either A) they weren't prepared to stay connected with us as we elevate to our new level, or B) we weren't prepared to stay connected with them as they elevate to their new level.

The third D is for divorce, which was one thing that hurt me the most because I was not as successful as some of my peers in my marriage. I feel that the reason being was that I didn't love my wife the way God intended me to love her, and for some time, the failure of that ate at me.

Fourth is destruction, which happened at every turn in the relationships that I attempted to have with a woman. Because I didn't have a real relationship with God, I couldn't have a real relationship with His child and would perhaps destroy them, leading into total destruction. Now that we've seen the bad, let's go to the 4 good D's.

First, we have diligent. Hebrews 11:6 tells us, "But without faith it is impossible to please him: for he that cometh to God must believe that he is, and that he is a rewarder of those who diligently seek him."

Second, we're devoted, something that we have to become in Christ once we've received Him in each and every day of our lives. Psalms 119:38 tells us to "Stablish thy word unto thy servant, who is devoted to thy fear."

Because we have the reverence, fear and love of God, we're devoted to do His will.

Third, as well as the fourth D, are delight and desire. Now that we've established a real relationship with God, Psalms 37:4 tells us this: "Delight thyself also in the Lord; and he shall give thee the desires of thine heart." So, as you see, God has taken 4 bad D's and replaced them with 4 good D's so that His will is to be done in our lives.

So, stay diligent and devoted, and He will make you delighted and fulfill your greatest desire and that you would be one in serving God for the world to see!

Waymaker
Daniel 6:22

God, being so wise, knows when we need His help, even when we don't. He goes by many names, but the name that I have for Him is Waymaker, because He is God, He can make a way out of no way! And when man says 'No!', God says 'Yes!', and God always has the final word in anything and everything. There are so many times in our lives where He becomes a waymaker, just as there are times in the Bible that He has become a waymaker.

You can begin in the Garden of Eden in Genesis 2:21-22: "And the Lord God caused a deep sleep to fall upon Adam, and he slept; and he took one of his ribs, and closed up the flesh instead thereof; And the rib, which the Lord God had taken from man, made he a woman, and brought her unto the man."

In this, God made a way for Adam to obtain the helpmate that he needed in the Garden of Eden! We continue in Genesis 6:13-14: "And God said unto Noah, 'The end of all flesh is come before me; for the earth is full of violence through them; and, behold, I will destroy them with the earth. Make thee an ark of gopherwood; rooms shalt thou make in the ark, and shalt pitch it within and without with pitch." In here, God made a way for Noah to escape the flood and repopulate the earth. Further on, in Genesis 19:15-16 in the destruction of Sodom and Gomorrah: "And when the morning arose, then the angels hastened Lot, saying, Arise, take thy wife, and thy two daughters, which are here; lest thou be consumed in the iniquity of the city. And while he lingered, the man laid hold upon his hand, and upon the hand of his wife, and upon the hand of his two daughters; the Lord being merciful unto him: and they brought him forth, and set him without the city." That's how He became a waymaker for Lot and his family.

  Now, we look further in Exodus 14:21-22. As Moses led God's people out of Egypt, but Pharaoh wouldn't let them go easy, he chased them down and thought to be trapped at the Red Sea. "And Moses stretched out his hand over the sea; and the Lord caused the sea to go back by a strong east wind all that night, and made the sea dry land, and the waters were divided. And the children of Israel went into the midst of the sea upon the dry ground: and the waters were a wall unto them on their right and,

and on their left." He became a waymaker once again for his children, but as we continue on in 1st Samuel 17:49, in what is considered the greatest upset in history, but then again, nothing is an upset if God is in it... when David had faced off against Goliath: "And David put his hand in his bag, and took thence a stone, and slang it, and smote the Philistine in his forehead, that the stone sunk into his forehead; and he fell upon his face to the earth. So David prevailed over the Philistine with a sling and with a stone and smote the Philistine and slew him; but there was no sword in the hand of David."

He proved yet again, this time thru David, to be a waymaker for His children, and as His children, we should look to God to make a way in every aspect of our lives. Another example is as he did with the three very familiar men, as it says in Daniel 3:26-27: "Then Nebuchadnezzar came near to the mouth of the burning fiery furnace, and spake, and said, 'Shadrach, Meshach and Abednego, ye servants of the most high God, come forth and come hither.' Then Shadrach, Meshach and Abednego, came forth of the midst of the fire. And the princes, governors, and captains, and the king's counsellors, being gathered together, saw these men, upon whose bodies the fire had no power, nor was a hair of their head singed, neither were their coats changed, nor the smell of fire had passed on them."

Truly, this is God being a waymaker to his most faithful children. And who can we say who was not as faithful as Daniel himself, as we continue in Daniel 6:22, when King Darius was tricked into signing a decree by jealous men, which in turn sent Darius into the lion's den searching for Daniel, when he found him Daniel exclaimed, "My God hath sent his angel, and hath shut the lions' mouth, that they have not hurt me: for as much as before him innocency was found in me; and also before thee, O king, have I done no hurt." This shows us once again, in what may consider certain death, God showed up and made a way for His children.

Now we come into a time when Christ had came and died, but His Apostles went forth to carry out His word. We see in Acts 5:19-20 as Peter and John were imprisoned a second time, "But the angel of the Lord by night opened the prison doors, and brought them forth, and said, 'Go, stand and speak in the temple to the people all the words of this life."

While God made a way before the eyes of the Sadducees that God's word was going to go out, meanwhile in Philippi, where Paul and Silas were caught and imprisoned on false accusations in Acts 16:25-26, it tells us, "And at midnight Paul and Silas prayed, and sang praises unto God: and the prisoners heard them. And suddenly there was a great earthquake, so that the foundations of the prison were shaken: and immediately all the doors were opened, and every one's bands were loosed." But it doesn't stop there. As the keeper went and saw that the doors were open, he feared that they had escaped. This for him was certain death. But Acts 16:30-31 tells us when Paul revealed himself to the keeper and letting him know that they didn't flee: "And brought them out, and said, 'Sirs, what must I do to be saved?' And they said, 'Believe on the Lord Jesus Christ, and thou shalt be saved and thy house." When Paul and Silas said that they were telling him of the ultimate waymaker, who is Jesus Christ.

As He said in John 14:6, "I'm the way, the truth and the life: no man can come to the father but by me." In this, He tells us that He is the waymaker, but also has another name, which is El Shaddi, meaning 'Pourer- Forth', which who Christ is--God poured into flesh.

He suffered, bled and died for our sins and sits on the right hand of God, to be a waymaker for us to come into heaven to meet God. But keep in His will and listen to Him and let Him have His way in your life and then you'll see how much of a waymaker He is!

Who's World Is This? Really?
Psalms 24:1

"The earth is the Lord's and the fullness thereof; the world, and they that dwell therein."

When David had said that, he knew who had overall ownership of this world. Even though Satan is considered "The prince of this world" in John 12:31, a prince has to give way to a king. No matter how big, how bad, how powerful and how popular the prince may be, that prince has to bow, clear a way or obtain permission from the king. If you continue to look in this Psalm, David lets you know who the king is, and I don't mean Elvis or Michael Jackson. They're just kings in their own minds. What do we have to do? Tell people about a real king, and if you don't know, read in verses 8 and 10 of Psalms 24 and there will be no doubt.

"And the fullness thereof;" can be two things to me: (1) it can mean heaven itself because of the splendor that emits from or the desire of it to be our final stop, knowing we will be in a place where we will be with our Father, and (2) God Himself, with grace, love, mercy, meekness and kindness which can quite literally be able to have a "fullness" to your heart, mind, soul and spirit. Because having the "fullness" of Jesus is perhaps the greatest "fullness" or a "high", from sex, alcohol, drugs, money, etc. But nothing or nobody can beat the "high" or "fullness" of Christ.

"The world, and they that dwell therein" is who we are, for we live in this world. We know that when this mortal body gives way, we will have a new body. Also, when Christ returns, He will have a new Heaven and a new Earth so that we may continue after the battle is over, to "dwell therein." But first, we must give ourselves to Jesus, allow Him rule in our lives, live as such, show others and tell the prince to go and let the king have his proper rule and throne in your life. Now, tell me, who's world is this? Really?

The 5th Bad D vs. The 5th Good D
Luke 4:18

I've told you about 'The 4 bad D's vs. the good D's'. I thought that I was done but the Spirit had shown me otherwise. I wasn't finished by a long-shot and I pray that I never will be when it comes to doing God's will, way, purpose and plan! I said earlier in the book that the 4 bad D's were (1) Death (2) Departure (3) Divorce and (4) Destruction, but there's one that I forgot to mention. If you let it, it will paralyze you not to do anything to glorify God, and that's Despair, which is an intransitive verb, meaning a verb that has or needs no complement to complete its meaning. In other words, it can stand there on its own like the way God can in our lives if we allow Him to.

Now despair is 2 Latin words: De-away plus sperare-to hope. It means to lose hope or abandon hope; be or become hopeless, and that is exactly what Satan wants us to feel and be: hopeless. Because when we're in storms, we feel like we have no hope, we feel sad, we feel depressed for Satan has put us in despair.

But now that you know about this one, here's what you do for that 5th bad D to get off of you. Use this 5th good D.

Now I've told you of the 4 good D's as well (1) Diligent (2) Devoted (3) Delight and (4) Desire. But this 5th D, as strong as despair is, this is stronger, which is Deliverance, for by prayer, fasting and seeking God, deliverance shall take you out of despair. Why? We look at Luke 4:18, as Jesus came back to Nazareth and read to those in the Synagogue out of the book of Esaias saying: "The Spirit of the Lord is upon me, because he hath anointed me to preach the gospel to the poor; he hath sent me to heal the brokenhearted, to preach deliverance to the captives, and recovering of sight to the blind, to set at liberty them that bruised."

God can and will deliver you out of each and every storm, even the storm of despair, so that you can be made that much stronger in God's will. To let a dying world know that Jesus lives and He can do for you what he's done for so many of us who live according to His word. So, as that spirit of despair comes upon you, call on Jesus and you shall be delivered, especially delivered by the real mailman, Jesus!

But Whose Side Are You On?
Psalms 124:2

"If it had not been the Lord who was on our side, when men rose up against us."

These are words of praise to a God who stands by us and for us in not only our brightest days, but our darkest days, and that's because He is a God that is worthy of anything and everything that we do. People feel that they just need God when everything is gone or almost gone, when all is lost, seeing what we can get from God, to do what we want and not what He wants. Because if we do what He wants, our lives will be better, finer, sweeter more in His will than ours. For we know if we do things in our own knowledge, strength and understanding, we do nothing but fail. But since we have, or supposed to have, an Almighty God that we're to serve and not the other way around, we live our life, or should live our life for Him and that Christ will be and shall be glorified in our lives.

We, at times, present company included, put God in a box or make the attempt to analyze, pick apart, scan with a magnifying glass all the things God has and will do for us.

We tried to take the goodness, glory and wondrous power that God produces and try to bottle it up and put it in a corner. But the real thing is that there is nothing any of us can do to contain the spirit when it falls upon us. As Paul wrote in his letter to the Thessalonians in 1st Thessalonians 5:16 to 23, we're supposed to "Rejoice evermore, Pray without ceasing, In everything give thanks: for this is the will of God in Christ Jesus concerning you, Quench not the Spirit, Despise not prophesyings, Prove all things; Hold fast that which is good, Abstain from all appearance of evil, And the very God of peace sanctify you wholly; and I pray God your whole spirit and soul and body be preserved blameless unto the coming of our Lord Jesus Christ."

But these things we don't do, present company included, but notice these following words I've Just said, not halfway, but totally and these words are: evermore, without ceasing, everything, quench not, prove, hold, abstain, wholly and finally whole spirit and soul. Just as God is on our side the very nano second that you've taken Him into your life as your savior and master.

The truth is, if God didn't work for us in our lives, we wouldn't do or say anything. Mind you, we would just be working in flesh, and that isn't on God's side. God's life isn't when we want it or need it, but 24-7-4-12 we're supposed to be and stay on His side.

Now, just as David said this with much joy because he was taken away from such a thing that only God can take him out, if you need help, look in that same Psalms in verse 8 and that is where your help is. So, tell God and tell others whose side you're on and then they will know the real side to be on.

Please Don't Cry
John 19:30

As I begin this with tears in my eyes, my heart and mouth filled with praise to Almighty God, who is powerful, but humble, slow to anger but quick to love...who sees, hears and knows all to insure, like the father that he is, His children are well. No one knows when, no one knows where we will be when God requires your soul. You could be sleeping in the evening, walking down the street, driving your car, etc., but when He does, please don't cry.

Please don't cry when God has told you that it's over, because if we're living the life like Jesus, then like Him, we can say as He hung in John 19:30, "When Jesus therefore had received the vinegar, he said 'It is finished:' and he bowed his head and gave up the ghost." Because remember, if you're living a life for Jesus and be like Jesus, the only thing that is finished is the work that is here, so please don't cry.

Please don't cry because I'm being taken to be with God. Remember Jesus' example in Luke 23:46: "And when Jesus had cried with a loud voice, he said 'Father into thy hands I commend my spirit: and having said thus, he gave up the ghost." So, I tell you, what better place can I or anyone be than in the hands of God? So please don't cry. Please don't cry, because as you hold my home going. It's going to be a beautiful day, despite what the weather will be. The beauty of that day will shine.

But please don't cry, for as the preacher ask for your hand and give God your heart and you don't because of what Satan is doing. Then I'll cry but it won't be too late. But don't wait too long to do it, because if you do, I'll cry. To those that God knows haven't yet given their lives to Him, please do and then we can be together again praising and having a good time. But to my brothers and sisters who've accepted Jesus in their lives, it's not goodbye, but rather, see you later because I'll be waiting for you once your earthly work is done and we will have fun forever and forever more. So please don't cry!

Send Me
Isaiah 6:8

"Also I heard the voice of the Lord, saying, 'Whom shall I send, and who will go for us?' Then said I 'Here am I; send me."

Do you hear Him? If you do, ask Him what He desires of you as He did with Samuel. In 1st Samuel 3:10, it reads, "And the Lord came and stood, and called as at other times, 'Samuel, Samuel.' Then Samuel answered, 'Speak; for thy servant heareth." For He wants to send you, with the gift or gifts that He has given to you, to show the people that are of the world what God and His word are all about. We have been given a commission, known as the Great Commission, which is found in Matthew 28:19-20, where Jesus spoke to the disciples, that they should "Go ye therefore, and teach all nations, baptizing them in the name of the Father, and of the Son, and of the Holy Ghost: Teaching them to observe all things whatsoever I have commanded you: and, lo, I am with you always, even unto the end of the world."

We also know that, as we take Christ as Lord of our lives, under the Great Commission we are to teach each and every person all about the gospel. Even when we don't go about and teach, our walk in the world, as well as our talk, is to show what God really is about because only God can take a little and make it more than we ever can.

As we look further on, God did not waste any time when in Isaiah 6:9-10 after the prophet made his intentions known: "And he said 'Go, and tell the people, Hear ye indeed, but understand not; and see ye indeed, but perceive not. Make the heart of this people fat, and make their ears heavy, and shut their eyes, lest they see with their eyes, hear with their ears, and understand with their heart, and convert, and be healed."

People do hear a lot of things and don't understand everything that they hear and see, but when they know that which is truth from God, it makes the heart happy, just as when a person for the first time is told that Jesus Christ loves them. It's that truth which makes their hearts happy and enables them to see and hear things from God that they had never heard of or saw before, because they had been blinded and drowned out by sin and the sickness of Satan that makes them think that those things that are sinful are acceptable and the things of God are unacceptable.

It should be the opposite. We, who are here by God's grace and mercy, are truly sent to remove the blinders and mufflers of darkness and expose it to God's saving light. Being human, we have a tendency to ask the same question that Isaiah asked in 6:11, but God immediately answered him when Isaiah spoke: "Then said I, 'Lord, how long?' and he answered, 'Until the cities be wasted without inhabitant, and the houses without man, and the land be utterly desolate." How long that is? Only God knows and I don't think he has told anyone as of yet. So, should God come to you as He did to Isaiah, I pray that your answer will be the same as his, as he said to the Lord, "Here am I; send me."

Sent To Save
John 3:17

"For God sent not his Son into the world to condemn the world; but that the world through him might be saved."

These are the words of Jesus as he spoke to a certain Pharisees named Nicodemus, who decided to speak to the Savior at night, to avoid any controversy. To have the Son of God speak these words, as powerful as they are, the only thing we all can and should say is, "I'm so glad that he didn't." If we stop and think, and really see those words, I'm sure you would say that. Why? Because if you look at the word condemn, you'll see why. I, for one, feel that nobody wants to be condemned.

Condemn means to pronounce judicial sentence against Those who are unsaved will be before the Lord in judgment, and have not their name been written in the Lamb's book of life, they shall be condemned to hell for all eternity. But Jesus did as He was sent to do: to tell all about the wonderfulness, grace, love and glory of God, and alas in the end, He suffered, bled and died between two thieves.

Now, if Jesus was guilty of any crime, it would be stealing; stealing souls to escape the damnation and the condemnation of Hell. But today that's our job. So, if it's a crime, then I'll pronounce myself guilty.

Jesus was hung and mocked on the cross, as written in Matthew 27:39-43: "And they that passed by reviled him, wagging their heads, And saying 'Thou that destroyest the temple, and buildest it in 3 days, save thyself.' 'If thou be the Son of God, come down from the cross.' Likewise also the chief priests mocking him, with the scribes and elders, said 'He saved others; himself he cannot save. If he be the King of Israel, let him now come down from the cross, and we will believe him. He trusted in God; let him deliver him now, if he will have him: for he said, 'I am the Son of God.'"

What words of insults to the one man who's able to take them from eternal damnation to eternal life! Having heard these words, Jesus could've done as they asked; (1) come down from the cross, then (2) removes the nail prints from his hands and feet, (3) remove the crown he was forced to wear, (4) healed his pierced side, but that's just the light stuff, (5) be so enraged by these people, after showing them how to live, crack the sky, and (6) call down angels from heaven and destroy them all. That's truly being condemned. But the only thing that truly kept Jesus on the cross was obedience, because had He done those things, he wouldn't have been doing God's will. Instead, he would've done what Satan had wanted and would've achieved total victory. But Jesus, being the Son of God that he is, hung on that rugged cross because of the obedience to God the Father, to save this world. Two things I leave you with, (1) Can we have that type of obedience to God as Jesus did? (2) And aren't you glad that he truly was sent to save?!

Saved By Grace
Ephesians 2:8

"For by grace are ye saved through faith; and that not of yourselves: it is the gift of God:"

Paul writes this in his letter to the people of Ephesus to explain to them that it is not what they do that has gotten them the things they had, but what God has given to them just by being God. Now the word grace is a noun which comes from the Latin word Gratia, meaning favor and has quite a few definitions. I'll go over some with you: (1) Beauty or harmony of motion form or manner, in which 2nd Corinthians 1:12 lets us know that, "For our rejoicing is this, the testimony of our conscience, that in simplicity and godly sincerity, not with fleshly wisdom, but by the grace of God, we have had our conversation in the world, and more abundantly to you-ward."

(2) The act of showing favor, in which Paul tells us in 2nd Corinthians 8:9 that, "For ye know the grace of our Lord Jesus Christ, that, though he was rich, yet for your sakes he became poor, that ye through his poverty might be rich." Jesus already had it all, but in order for us to

understand God, he had Jesus become a commoner, to be accepted by all men.

(3) Clemency and mercy, which Jesus showed when He died for our sins at Calvary, that Peter told us in Acts 15:11: "But we believe that through the grace of the Lord Jesus Christ we shall be saved, even as they." Do you think that is enough grace for anyone?

Not only those things we have by grace, but as it was explained earlier about riches, we are rich in grace as well, as Paul tells Timothy in 2nd Timothy 2:1: "Thou therefore, my son, be strong in the grace that is in Christ Jesus." For this in itself will give us the strength to endure. With fasting and prayer, you too will be strong in grace. But remember, we cannot think or say that we hate sinners, but just that we hate the sins that they commit because we too are sinners. But when we have answered the call of Jesus Christ, we became sinners who were saved by grace.

I Have the Power
2nd Timothy 1:7

"For God hath not given us the spirit of fear; but of power, and of love, and of a sound mind."

These words Paul writes to his young charge Timothy in expressing his love to him while being imprisoned in Rome, encouraging him to continue the work that was laid out for him by Paul. In just this one piece of scripture, Paul has told Timothy 4 very important things, and I feel that we should take them to be important as well.

First, Paul begins with, "For God hath not given us the spirit of fear," because fear is not what God is all about. Yes, we're supposed to have a healthy and revering fear of God, but not to the point where we can't ask or say anything to Him. We're to give God the same healthy fear as we give our parents, grandparents, extended family, etc. but not to be frightened of Him. You see, fear is one of Satan's biggest weapons, because once you have fear working on and against you, it can leave you frozen. And then all it takes is one good push and it's all over.

Second, Paul tells him "But of power," the power to do the work that was predestined, not only in Timothy's life, but in your life, my life and anyone else's life that God has touched. As Paul says in 2nd Corinthians 4:7, "But we have this treasure in earthen vessels, that the excellency of the power may be of God, and not of us." Since we, who are the children of God have the power, we need to use this power in the glory of the Lord to keep Satan from our homes, children, families, marriage, jobs, etc. and put him where he belongs; under us to stomp him down like the pest that he is.

Third, Paul says, "And of love," but as Tina Turner once said, "What's love got to do with it?" The answer is plenty because first, in 1st John 4:8, it says, "He that loveth not knoweth not God; for God is love." Second, if it wasn't for love, none of us would be here because it states in John 3:16, "For God so loved the world, that he gave his only begotten Son, that whosoever believeth in him should not perish, but have everlasting life." And that's what love got to do with it!

Fourth and finally, Paul says, "And of a sound mind." Because with a sound mind, we should praise, exalt, glorify, honor and magnify God to the highest, just as Paul said in Philippians 2:2: "Fulfil ye my joy, that ye be likeminded, having the same love, being of one accord, of one mind." Now that we have all of these things, can we say together that 'I have the power!'

How Sweet It Is
Psalms 100:5

"For the Lord is good; his mercy is everlasting; and his truth endureth to all generations."

Hmmmmm! What was the psalmist thinking of when he said this? Praise? Surly! But I'm sure there's more to it, as he begins, "For the Lord is good." Truly He is, for we can attest to it, as the elder saints would say, "When I think about the goodness of the Lord..." or according to Nahum 1:7, "The Lord is good, a strong hold in the day of trouble; and he knoweth them that trust in him," which is why He's good.

"His mercy is everlasting;". First let's see; mercy is a disposition to be kind, forgiving, or helpful, which describes some of the attributes of God. Psalms 103:17 says, "But the mercy of the Lord is from everlasting to everlasting upon them that fear him, and his righteousness unto children's children;". And who but God can truly see "from everlasting to everlasting?" "And his truth endureth to all generations?"

Jesus says in Matthew 24:35, "Heaven and earth shall pass away, but my words shall not pass away." Since God's word is found in the Bible and is based on truth and has lasted for many generations, for as long as God's word reigns supreme, it shall endure.

"For the Lord is good." Aren't you glad He is? "His mercy is everlasting." Doesn't that make you happy? "His truth endureth to all generations." How sweet it is!

Holiday Intermission

Lord, everyday in and with you is like a holiday.

You're like New Year's Day because

you start everything off.

Valentine's Day, because of your love for us.

Good Friday, because you died for us.

Easter, because you rose for us as you said.

Fourth of July, because you set us free to be what you

want us to be.

Labor Day, because the true labor is the

love you have for us.

Thanksgiving, because we give thanks to you

for all you've done.

Christmas, because you gave us the greatest gift of all:

You!!

Whole Heart
Psalms 111:1

"Praise ye the Lord. I will praise the Lord with my whole heart, in the assembly of the upright, and in the congregation."

Psst! Psst! Hey you! Yeah, you reading this! You want to know a secret? I thought you would. You want to know how to make God happy? This is all you have to do to make God happy: Praise Him! You see, God enjoys our praises. He enjoys them so much that He blesses those who praise Him, especially those who do it from the heart. Anybody can give superficial praise, but the praise God looks for comes from the heart, because if you stop and think, God doesn't just bless us halfway. So why should we give Him halfway praise? Because if we were blessed by how we praise God, we probably wouldn't have half the blessings we have now. Let's be real! A lot of times we (myself included) don't really give whole-hearted praise, but still God doesn't just bless us halfway. So, let's give Him the praise with our whole heart.

It doesn't matter if you're in your car, house, church, job, etc., give it to God because He deserves it all. As the old saying goes: 'when praises go up, blessings come down!' And if they're truly from the heart, there will be blessings that much better! But let's not stop there; there are 4 things that we can and should do with our whole heart.

First, in obedience, where Psalms 119:2 says, "Blessed are they that keep his testimonies, and that seek him with the whole heart." For we're to be obedient with our whole heart.

Second, we're to do it in repentance, where in Joel 2:12 as he speaks of God's judgment to the people of Zion in saying this: "Therefore also now, saith the Lord, Turn ye even to me with all of your heart, and with fasting, and with weeping, and with mourning." For we're to repent with our whole heart.

Third, there are times that we don't, but when we're in prayer, we must give God our whole heart, as Jeremiah 29:13 says as he speaks to the people of Babylon: "And ye shall seek me, and find me, when ye shall search for me with all your heart."

Because if you don't seek God with a whole-hearted prayer, you will never, ever find Him. Oh, He's there, but you won't feel His holy presence and that's bad.

Fourth and most importantly, with trust, where Proverbs 3:5 says, "Trust in the Lord with all thine heart; and lean not unto thine own understanding." But when you do this, do you know what that is called? Faith, because we put so much of our obedience, we repent to, go in prayer and put trust in a God that can do anything but lie and fail. A former NBA superstar holds this message that Paul gives to the church of Corinth very near and dear to his heart, which is in 2nd Corinthians 5:7. It says, "For we walk by faith, not by sight:", and that's exactly what we do when we love, live, and testify for our soon and coming king Jesus Christ with our whole heart!

God's Hammer
Jeremiah 23:29

During this brief stay we have on this world that God has created for His creation, we're here to do what His will is, according to His way so that He may be glorified. But there are times when we are at war, and although we do have weapons, we don't even know how to use them. For Paul has written in Ephesians 6:12, "For we wrestle not against flesh and blood but against principalities, against powers, against the rulers of darkness of this world, against spiritual wickedness in high places."

With Satan planning each and every point in the battles against us all, from the president to the welfare mother, we are all being subjected to Satan's blows. But don't be discouraged. God didn't leave us defenseless in this battle, for 2nd Corinthians 10:4 tells us, "For the weapons of our warfare are not carnal, but mighty through God to the pulling down of strong holds". We also have protection that we can find in Ephesians 6:14-17 and a very special offensive weapon found in Hebrews 4:12: "For the word of God is quick, and powerful, and sharper than any two edged sword, piercing even to the dividing asunder of soul and spirit, and of the joints and marrow, and is a discerner of the thoughts and intents of the heart."

Not only do we have a sword, but we also have 2 other objects in our fight against the enemy as it's recorded in Jeremiah 23:29: "Is not my word like as a fire? saith the Lord; and like a hammer that breaketh the rock in pieces?" Now we have 3 weapons. How should we use them? First, we use the sword to cut thru Satan's lies, then we use the fire to burn away his deceptions, and finally the hammer to break down the barriers that Satan uses to try and separate us from our blessings that God has for us. But finally, we have the most important weapon of all: Prayer. Without it, (1) we cannot communicate with our heavenly Father, (2) we wouldn't have the preservation to combat the enemy as Paul explains in Ephesians 6:18: "Praying always with all prayer and supplication in the Spirit, and watching there unto with all perseverance and supplication for all saints."

With these weapons laid out for us and with God's help, we can and will defeat the defeated foe known as Satan. So, when Satan tries to put up walls around you, always remember that you can destroy them all with God's hammer!

No Confusion
Psalms 71:1

"In thee, O Lord, do I put my trust: let me never be put to confusion."

What the psalmist says is true, because in God is where we should always put our trust at and in. When we put trust in the things of this world or in this world, then we leave ourselves open to so many things here, that it would be against us rather than for us. Trust is something that is dear and precious to us because it is something we put everything into, and without it, we have nothing. The things in this world we cannot ever put our trust in, but only in the hands of a loving, powerful and forgiving God. The trust that you have will always endure.

"Let me never be put to confusion." Confusion is an act or instance of confusing or the quality or state of being confused. Confusion is what Satan wants to put us in so we cannot (1) have a clear understanding of God's word, (2) clearly hear that small still voice, (3) know what His will is for you. The third reason is very important, not that the other two are not, but if we don't know what God's will is in our life, we will be wandering in confusion.

Paul tells us in 1st Corinthians 14:33: "For God is not the author of confusion, but of peace, as in all the churches of the saints." And those that do dwell and delight in God's will and God's way are saints.

Confusion is nothing more than another tool Satan uses against us in our lives as we continue to strive and drive in the long and enduring race that we run. We hold onto God and allow Him to be our strength and the true light on our pathways, that we may hopefully show those who have not taken Jesus Christ in their lives who God really is and that we can do it with no confusion!

Count It
James 1:2

"My brethren, count it all joy when ye fall into divers temptation;"

When you watch a basketball game and you see your favorite player make a shot beyond the norm while being fouled and it goes in, the referee makes the signal to count the basket. But what does this have to do with what James said? Quite a bit actually, because just as that player try it and if it comes out good, even if it should start rocky or difficult, count it anyway! So, if the car breaks down, count it! You lose your job, count it! If you see everything all about you seems bad, count it! Because as Jesus walks with you, talks with you, stays with you at all times, then you can have the joy that God and God alone has and gives it to you.

Paul has said in Romans 8:28, "And we know that all things work together for good to them that love God, to them who are the called according to His purpose." It will be that much more of a learning experience to be more in God. Even in those times that you go through, God is still working it out, shaping it out, molding it out, craving it out and breaking it out for the good that God has for you.

But there are two things that are attached to it: (1) it's "to them that love God", because if you think for one second that God is going to do something for you and you have no love for him, you are sadly mistaken. God does each and everything good, bad or indifferent and if we try to take the credit for what God does, beware for as Moses wrote in Deuteronomy 6:15: "(For the Lord thy God is a jealous God among you)' lest the anger of the Lord thy God be kindled against thee, and destroy thee from off the face of the earth."

(2) It's also "to them who are the called according to his purpose." Because if it's not done to God's purpose, it's not going to get done. You see, man does things for his own purpose and it's not done for His purpose because we're not looking to God and seeing what His true purpose is. So, try to put up your shot for it may go in towards the purpose of God and the glory of Jesus Christ. Then you can go and count it!

<u>*The Fulfilling Power of God*</u>
Matthew 5:6

"Blessed are they which do hunger and thirst after righteousness: for they shall be filled."

Do you remember the times when you were in the world, when you were hungry and thirsty for those things that were in the world? You sat down and ate out of the salad bowl of greed, which was sprinkled and colored with envy? Eating the bread of destruction? Having a large portion of flesh, decorated with sex and glazed over with lust? A side dish of drugs and finally drinking it all down with alcohol? You had all of that and still you were not filled. Why? Because you were hungry and thirsty for the wrong thing.

So, what are we supposed to be hungry and thirsty for? Well in this part of His sermon on the mount, Jesus specifically tells us what we are supposed to be hungry and thirsty for to be filled: righteousness! But what is righteousness you ask? Good question! Righteousness, which comes from righteous, is an adjective created from two Old English words: Right, meaning right, and Wis, meaning wise is (1) conforming to a standard of right and justice; virtuous, in which Proverbs 31:10-30 tells us all about a virtuous woman. Also, Romans 12:2 tells us, "And be not conformed to this world: but be ye transformed by the renewing of your mind, that ye may prove what is that good, and acceptable, and perfect, will of God."

(2) morally right; equitable: a righteous act. But who can we ever say was truly righteous? None but Jesus Christ! This is why He is called Jehovah-Tsidkenu, which means The Lord our Righteousness, for which He truly is. When you get a portion of God, Psalms 34:8 tells us, "O taste and see that the lord is good: blessed is the man that trusteth in him." Not only that, but there's an added bonus. Once you do taste Him, John 6:35 says, "And Jesus said unto them, 'I am the bread of life: he that cometh to me shall never hunger; and he that believeth on me shall never thirst." So, sit at the table, eat, drink and believe and you too can truly enjoy and take in the fulfilling power of God!

It's Only My Pride
Proverbs 16:18

"Pride goeth before destruction, and an haughty spirit before a fall."

It's apparent that Solomon knew then, what we now know today, what pride can and will do to a person, because if we take pride in the things we do in our lives, instead of letting God receive the credit in our lives, then we will be destroyed or fall. Haughty is an adjective, meaning to exhibit great disdain for others. Don't you notice that when a person shows a lot of pride in themselves, they have a tendency of looking down at others, trying to make themselves appear to be more than who or what they are? But what we should do is remember where everything comes from.

Paul explains this as he writes in Ephesians 2:8-9 by saying, "For by grace are ye saved through faith; and that not of yourselves: it is the gift of God: Not of works, lest any man should boast." So, what gives us the right to boast or brag about what we have or what we do?

Because it's the Lord that has done it for us and not towards us, so keep your eyes stayed on Jesus and you won't have any need for pride.

But then again, there are other examples of pride as well. In Proverbs 8:13, where Solomon clearly explains how the Lord feels about pride and what goes along with it, he says, "The fear of the Lord is to hate evil: pride, and arrogancy, and the evil way, and the forward mouth, do I hate."

As we look further in Proverbs 11:2, it reads, "When pride cometh, then cometh shame: but with the lowly is wisdom." That's when you feel you know the answer and not research it and follow it through, then it turns out that you were wrong. This is when you feel the shame. And the real shame is to take away from God what He has done for us and it is not giving to Him the glory that He richly deserves. Because then and only then, when we lift up the blood-stained banner of Jesus Christ and glorify God, is when we can have the real joy in what we do in our lives.

Did Jesus take pride in dying for our sins? I believe the answer to that question is no, because in the Garden of Gethsemane, Matthew 26:39 says, "And he went a little farther, and fell on his face, and prayed, saying, O my Father, if it be possible, let this cup pass from me: nevertheless not as I will, but thou wilt." But because of His obedience, He still went forward, and I, for one, am happy that He didn't take any pride in it. So, next time you have that spirit of self-exaltation, and the Holy Spirit bursts your bubble, just remember you're not hurt. But just tell what really hurts is only my pride!

<u>Like A Tree</u>
Psalms 1:3

"And he shall be like a tree planted by the rivers of water, that bringeth forth his fruit in his season; his leaf also shall not wither; and whatsoever he doeth shall prosper."

Don't you know that we're like trees? How? Well, like a tree, we start off as a seed, for we are the seed of our parents. Like a tree, we were nurtured and were able to grow. Like a tree, we have roots to go back into our family line, to know who we are and where we come from. But when we had accepted Jesus Christ into our lives, that's when the Lord's seed was planted into our hearts and minds. We also grew because we allowed ourselves to be nurtured and grow under the Word of God, which is the Bible.

Like a tree, we have roots. These are rooted and grounded on the only thing that can and shall preserve us all in good times and in bad, no matter what the storms of life throw at you. You will never be uprooted as long as long as you are rooted in God's Word.

Like a tree, we have branches that reach towards the sky, drinking the warmth of the sun. But our branches reach out towards the sky so that we may be able to reach closer to God.

Like this tree, we're "planted by the rivers of water" to get our strength, but we now have a better and different water supply, and that is Jesus Christ. In John 4:13-14, when the woman at the well spoke to him, it says, "Jesus answered and said unto her, 'Whosoever drinketh of this water shall thirst again: But whosoever drinketh of the water that I shall give him shall be in him a well of water springing up into everlasting life.'"

"That bringeth forth his fruit in his season;" Jesus had told us in Matthew 12:33 that we "either make the tree good, and his fruit good; or else make the tree corrupt, and his fruit corrupt: for the tree is known by his fruit." But it's only in God's will when that fruit will come.

"His leaf also shall not wither;" because as we grow in age, Psalms 92:14 tells us that, "They shall still bring forth fruit in old age; they shall be fat and flourishing;".

So, get under grandma and grandpa if they are living a life for God and partake of their fruit while the Lord has them here, for they've been kept by His hand so that their "leaf also shall not wither."

"And whatsoever he doeth shall prosper," but only if you do it to the glory of the Lord will that happen. Just as Moses did with Israel in the land of Moab with the covenant that the Lord commanded in Deuteronomy 29:9, for them to "keep therefore the words of this covenant, and do them, that ye may prosper in all that ye do." Doesn't it feel good to prosper in God's will? So, let yourself be a willing vessel to Jesus Christ. Be in prayer and learn His Word, and in due season, you in turn will bear good fruit. And be rotted and grounded, so that the storms of life will not bring you down. Then you too can stand strong for God, just like a tree!

The Power of Praise
Psalms 150:6

Praise is what we are to give to God, for He and He alone is deserving of it because of the things that He has done in our lives. Praise has so much unspeakable power. It's so awesome. It's confusing to man, but not to those who he calls his children. Praise can hold, help and heal you through all types of situations that we will never, ever understand, because if we had the true understanding of God, then what use would we have of Him?

We're told to "let everything that hath breath praise the Lord. Praise ye the Lord." Since He has given you the power to draw breath, don't you think for one minute that you should give Him praise for that? Praise is what we feed God because He delights in it, for when we feed Him, he in turn feeds us with riches and blessings which we cannot explain or understand. David has told us what we must do when he said in Psalms 34:1 that "I will bless the Lord at all times: his praise shall continually be in my mouth." With the mouth, we give God what he deserves. With the mouth we are heard by God. But not only with the mouth, but with the heart as well.

Psalms 111:1 tells us we're to "Praise ye the Lord. I will praise the Lord with my whole heart, in the assembly of the upright and in the congregation." It doesn't matter where you are, praise is what you should do and to share it with those who need, have and hold onto it. Praise glorifies Him for who He is, which is El Elyion which means the "Most High", for that is what He truly is and there's none higher than God.

Did you know that Hallelujah is the highest praise that we can give to God? Don't you think that he's deserving of our best? Our ultimate? Our highest that we can give Him? Remember when you focus mind, body and spirit unto Jesus Christ and what He has done for you, you will truly know the power of praise!

Prisoner or Free Man: Which One Are You?
Matthew 18:18

"Verily I say unto you, Whatsoever ye shall bind on earth shall be bound in heaven: and whatsoever ye shall loose on earth shall be loose in heaven."

Imagine that! We have the power to either bind or loose things not just here on earth, but in heaven as well. But the binding began when Adam and Eve ate of the fruit of the tree of knowledge and good and evil, thus being cast out of the Garden of Eden. Since then, man has been born into this world bound, bound in a prison called sin, as Psalms 51:5 speaks of: "Behold, I was shaped in iniquity; and in sin did my mother conceive me."

Thus, we have become prisoners in sin, to go against God's Word, not to do His will, turn away from His voice, locked up, tied down, put away in a place where we had no real choice to be in at all. Why? Because we are bound. We're bounded by a warden who wouldn't want us to do what God wants from us, what He desires from us, and what He cherishes from us. We're bounded by one that God himself threw out of heaven because of his lust of power. That warden's name is Satan!

You know, it's not too hard to believe, but the most prettiest thing around can be the most ugliest! Why? You see Lucifer, or as we also know him as Satan, was an angel. Not just any angel, but the number one angel second only to God. But then, he just did not want to be the number one angel. He wanted to be the number one man in heaven, which isn't what he was intended to be. So, he gathered one-third of heaven and staged a rebellion.

God, being all-knowing, knew of this and tossed Lucifer and his followers out of heaven and down towards earth. From there Lucifer, lost his beauty that he had in heaven with the ugliness of sin, which he wants and desires to keep us in its darkening grip. He attempts to bind down the gifts that God gives to us, hold back the blessings that God has for us and mostly, keeps God away from us. Is this the type of prisoner you want to be?

But how do we become free of this prison? We become free when we make the choice! The choice that we are not going to stay in the prison of sin, wear the chains of iniquity, and no longer to be bounded in mind, body and spirit by our warden Satan, but released by the lawyer in our life who God himself sent here to release us from these things, and that lawyer's name is Jesus Christ!

He came down in the form of a man to be tempted, suffered, bled, lived, breathed, ate, slept and finally to die as a man, to know (1) what it is to be a man, (2) to be the one to post our bail, and (3) to leave the prison that Satan rules. When we accept Jesus Christ into our hearts and our lives, we become free: free to do His will, free to listen to that small still voice and mostly, free to see in his Word what He has for us if we obey him. Jesus tells us in his exchange with the Jews in John 8:36 that, "If the Son therefore shall make you free, ye shall be free indeed."

Free and loose, to use the gifts God has given you, free to receive the blessings that He has for you, and free to know the love that He has for you. Now, with all of the things God has for us and wants to do for us, wouldn't you want to be free? The decision is yours to make. Now I ask you once more: prisoner or free man, which one are you?

Hiding in Plain Sight
John 1:10

"He was in the world, and the world was made by him, and the world knew him not."

Do you ever have those days when you lay your keys down on the living room table, and then when you are ready to leave, they're not there? You rip up the bedroom, tear down the bathroom, toss through the kitchen, throw the dining room to the left and the family room to the right, and finally you sit down back in the living room and there they are, looking right at you! That's the way Jesus was when He came down to earth. He was there but nobody really knew. Some had an ideal on who he was, but not the whole idea. He went about performing miracles, doing things no one else has ever done and never will only because He is God! Not even John the Baptist knew until after he baptized Jesus when he said in John 1:33-34, "And I knew him not: but he that sent me to baptize with water, the same said unto me, Upon whom thou shalt see the Spirit descending, and remaining on him, the same is he which baptizeth with the Holy Ghost. And I saw, and bare record that this is the Son of God."

Who else can turn waterpots of water into wine? Who else can tell you all about you without speaking to nobody else? Who else can heal a child just by speaking it and that child be in another city and be healed? Who else can speak light and there was light? Don't you think after everything was done during this timeframe, that these people would have figured out who Jesus was? Because nobody but God's son can be able to do the things that were done and done in a way that would have glorified God.

But still they bothered not to take heed to what Jesus said, even to the day when He hung on the cross and the people mocked him in Mark 15:31-32: "Likewise also the chief priests mocking said among themselves with the scribes, 'He saved others; himself he cannot save. Let Christ the King of Israel descend now from the cross, that we may see and believe. And they that were crucified with him reviled him." These were among some of the indignities that Christ suffered and there are others that we suffer also because of our walk in God. But don't worry, when things start happening to those that are of the world, who do they call upon first?

Because when they do, they will call you to get them out of the situation that they are in. Until then, we will be there, hiding in plain sight.

Have A Life
1 John 5:12

Every day, we go by wanting and wishing to have a good life and to live a good life. But let's get down to the bottom line, and that is, if you don't have Jesus Christ in your life, you will not have life, because only a life in Him is the thing that will make life great. Solomon has told us in Proverbs 12:28 that, "In the way of righteousness is life; and in the pathway thereof there is no death." If you have Jesus helping you live in the way of righteousness, you will have life.

And what must you do? Do as the lawyer stated when he spoke to Jesus in Luke 10:27-28: "And he answered and said 'Thou shalt love the Lord thy God with all thy heart, and what all thy strength, and with all thy mind; and thy neighbor as thyself. And he said unto him, 'Thou hast answered right: this do, and thou shalt live." We all know that it's hard, but if you have God guiding you in your life, you can do it, no matter what the situation may be! For when we go to judgment, we will be looked upon by God.

1st Corinthians 3:13 tells us, "Every man's work shall be made manifest: for the day shall declare it, because it shall be revealed by fire; and the fire shall try every man's work of what sort it is." So, ask yourself: What kind of works in your life do you want to have when you stand before God?

Even though life may present us with fearful things that Satan throws at you, remember God's grace, mercy and excellence, as David did when he spoke in Psalms 23:4: "Yea, though I walk through the valley of the shadow of death, I will fear no evil: for thou art with me; thy rod and thy staff they comfort me." Because when you have given your life to God, Satan will try to step in and may have your wife to leave you, husband to leave you, family to leave you, your friends, even your best friend, to leave you. But God will never leave you, even in your worst times!

He wants us to have a rich life. We can only have it with Christ, because Jesus tells us in John 10:10 that, "The thief cometh not, but for to steal, and to kill, and to destroy: I am come that they might have life, and that they might have it more abundantly." Now, who among us would not want that also?

But more than anything, you have to believe, because if you believe, John 3:36 lets us know that, "He that believeth on the Son hath everlasting life: and he that believeth not the Son shall not see life; but the wrath of God abideth on him." I know that I wish not His wrath be upon me, nor would I want it to be upon you, but the decision can only be made by you! Remember that, "He that hath the Son hath life; and he that hath not the Son of God hath not life." So, when you have Jesus in your life, you always will have a life!

Believe and See Not
John 20:29

"Jesus saith unto him, Thomas, because thou hast seen me, thou hast believed: blessed are they that have not seen, and yet have believed."

It's surprising for people to realize that there was actually one disciple in his group that felt they had to be there in order to believe in anything. Thomas was what I call a Missouri Christian, because he had to be shown instead of having the faith to believe that Jesus would rise again, as He said that he would. Now, the word believed is past tense from the word believe, which is a verb that comes from the Middle English word Beleven, which in turn, comes from the Old English word Gelefan, meaning 'to believe.'

There are quite a few definitions to the word believe: (1) to accept as true or real. Now, there are so many people in different religions and different walks of life who feel that the Bible, and all of the things that it contains, are not true and real. But there are too many things that have actually happened over the course of history that proves that the Bible is indeed true and real.

When the people were led out of Egypt and into the wilderness, although they had been blessed by God beyond all understanding, they did not believe. Moses wrote in Numbers 14:11, "And the Lord said unto Moses, 'How long will this people provoke me? And how long will it before they believe, for all the signs which I have shewed among them?" Shouldn't those things that have happened been enough for them to believe?

(2) To accept the truth, existence, worth, etc. of something. When we accept Jesus Christ and allow Him in our lives as truth, John 1:12 tells us, "But as many as received him, to them gave he power to become the sons of God, even to them that believe on his name." It's because of the acceptance of the truth and existence and worth of Jesus Christ that we have become the sons and daughters of God, who is also called Elohim, which means creator. For how can you not believe after seeing all that He has created?

(3) To have confidence; place one's trust: where in John 11:42, when Jesus is speaking in the trust that He has in God; "And I knew that thou hearest me always: but because of the people which stand by I said it, that they

may believe that thou hast sent me." He had just that much confidence in the Father, to allow His friend Lazarus to be raised from the dead.

    (4) To have religious faith. You see, faith is the main ingredient of believing because once you can believe is when faith kicks in for you. You can't believe if you don't have faith, which is why the woman that was sick for 12 years mentioned in Matthew 9:21, "For she said within herself, 'If I may but touch his garment, I shall be whole." It was that faith she had in Jesus that healed her, because Jesus came down here on earth to do God's work for all of those which He has called to be His children. For all of the things God has done and will do for you in your life, if you have not taken Him into your life, you can't afford to delay another second. Allow Jesus Christ to enter into your heart, then you will be able to know the power of God, and then be able to believe and see not!

www.ingramcontent.com/pod-product-compliance
Lightning Source LLC
Chambersburg PA
CBHW011407070526
44577CB00003B/401